NAILED IT!

Extreme ICE CROSS DOWNHILL

Virginia Loh-Hagan

45th Parallel Press

Published in the United States of America by Cherry Lake Publishing
Ann Arbor, Michigan
www.cherrylakepublishing.com

Content Adviser: Liv Williams, Editor, www.iLivExtreme.com
Reading Adviser: Marla Conn, ReadAbility, Inc.
Photo Credits: ©Ara1957/Dreamstime.com, cover, 1; ©Predrag Vuckovic/Red Bull Content Pool, 5; ©Andreas Langreiter/Red Bull Content Pool, 6; ©Predrag Vuckovic/Red Bull Content Pool, 8; ©Sebastian Marko/Red Bull Content Pool, 11; ©Victor5490/Dreamstime.com, 13; ©Scott Serfas/Red Bull Content Pool, 15; ©Jupiterimages/Thinkstock.com, 17; ©Joerg Mitter/Red Bull Content Pool, 19; ©IM_photo/Shutterstock.com, 21; ©Andreas Langreiter/Red Bull Content Pool, 23; ©Victor5490/Dreamstime.com, 25; ©Joerg Mitter/Red Bull Content Pool, 26; ©Andreas Langreiter/Red Bull Content Pool, 29; ©Trusjom/Shutterstock.com, multiple interior pages; ©Kues/Shutterstock.com, multiple interior pages

45th Parallel Press is an imprint of Cherry Lake Publishing.

Library of Congress Cataloging-in-Publication Data

Names: Loh-Hagan, Virginia.
Title: Ice cross downhill / by Virginia Loh-Hagan.
Description: Ann Arbor : Cherry Lake Publishing, [2016] | Series: Nailed it! | Includes bibliographical references and index.
Identifiers: LCCN 2015026819| ISBN 9781634704861 (hardcover) | ISBN 9781634705462 (pdf) | ISBN 9781634706063 (paperback) | ISBN 9781634706667 (ebook)
Subjects: LCSH: Skateboarding--Juvenile literature. | Extreme sports--Juvenile literature.
Classification: LCC GV859.8 .L64 2016 | DDC 796.22--dc23
LC record available at http://lccn.loc.gov/2015026819

ABOUT THE AUTHOR

Dr. Virginia Loh-Hagan is an author, university professor, former classroom teacher, and curriculum designer. When she went ice skating, she spent more time falling on the ice than skating. She lives in San Diego with her very tall husband and very naughty dogs. To learn more about her, visit www.virginialoh.com.

Table of Contents

1

Crash and Continue

Who is Kyle Croxall? What is ice cross downhill? Who is Marco Dallago? Who are some female ice cross downhill skaters?

Kyle Croxall skates down icy ramps. He skates over big jumps. He skates around sharp corners. He falls. He crashes. He won a lot. Then he lost a lot. But he worked hard.

He practices ice cross downhill or downhill skating. It combines ice hockey, downhill skiing, and in-line skating.

Skaters skate downhill on a walled, iced track. The track has sharp turns. It has high drops of more than 200 feet

(61 meters). It's between 1,400 and 2,000 feet (426.7 to 609.6 m) long. Skaters race four at a time.

Marco Dallago fights for the front positions. He's an ice cross downhill champion. He started skiing at age four. He started downhill skating at age 13. He built a training track. It's in a forest. It's close to his hometown. It's in Austria. It's 656 feet (200 m) long.

Downhill ice cross is a new sport.

Ice cross downhill skaters have endurance. They don't quit.

He said, "Forty or 50 seconds of skating downhill doesn't sound like a lot of effort. … It's as **exhausting** as anything you've ever experienced." That means it is tiring. But he keeps practicing.

Ice cross downhill is not for quitters.

Today, more women are doing ice cross downhill. Jacqueline Legere said it's an "amazing, insane sport."

It's easy to crash. She studies the ice conditions. She watches for other people wiping out. She stays on her feet.

NAILED IT!

Spotlight Biography: Fannie Desforges

Fannie Desforges is known as "Fearless Fannie." She's from Canada. She was captain of her university's women's ice hockey team. She's the second Canadian woman to win a Red Bull Crashed Ice competition. She plays ice hockey for the Montreal Stars. Growing up, she played ice hockey with boys. They wouldn't pass her the puck. She proved she was better. She outskated them. She trains a lot. She likes downhill ice skating. She said, "It's pretty crazy. You can't be scared. If you are scared, the track will eat you up." She would like to see more women enter the sport. She likes being a role model for other girls. She said, "This is a sport that gets you out of your comfort zone and allows athletes to reach a new level of difficulty."

Crashed Ice is the biggest downhill skating competition. One year, the course took 20 days to make.

Salla Kyhala competes with men. She said, "It's hard. But women are strong, too." She said, "We've proved that we're good skaters. We need to get women involved at all the races."

Elaine Topolnisky loves speed. She said, "The more we race, the better we get." Women are improving each year.

"We need to get women involved at all the races."

2

Fastest Sport on Skates

What do ice cross downhill skaters do? What are the tracks like? What do they wear? How did Sever Lundquist train? What skills do all downhill skaters need? What is ski cross?

Ice cross downhill is the fastest sport on skates. They start on a high ramp. It's three stories tall. They rush down an ice track. They race down a zigzagging course. They jump. They drop. They turn. They crash. They reach speeds of 40 miles (64 kilometers) per hour. The first skater to the bottom wins.

The track is steep and icy. It's like a giant slide. It has rolling bumps. It has big jumps. It has steep drops. It has **hairpin** turns. These turns are like sharp U-turns. There's lots of wind. No two courses are alike.

Downhill skaters may not slow down or stop other skaters. They can't hurt other skaters on purpose. They can't trip other skaters. They can't hold on to their clothes. They'll get kicked out of the race. But skaters still crash into each other. They also crash into objects.

Ice cross downhill skaters wear ice hockey gear. This is for protection. They wear full-face helmets. They wear

Many ice cross downhill skaters got inspired from watching it on television.

NAILED IT!

Advice from the Field: Cameron Naasz

Cameron Naasz is from Minnesota. He started playing ice hockey at age five. He was the first American to win an Ice Cross Downhill World Championship event. Earlier in that season, he lost to other skaters. He made many mistakes. He learned from his mistakes. He used that knowledge to win. Naasz practiced racing a lot. That was the hardest part for him. He wants to be in the top of every race. He said, "My advice to anyone coming into the sport would be to listen to the coaches during your first training sessions. Take in as much advice as you can from the experienced riders. And watch all the best riders very closely because it's all the little things they do that save you crucial time and speed on the track."

shoulder pads. They wear chest and back pads. They wear elbow pads. They wear pants with knee and leg pads. They wear gloves. They wear ice hockey skates.

Sever Lundquist climbed 84 metal steps. He reached the starting gate. He was 48 feet (14.6 m) above the ground. He took two steps. He flew downhill. To practice, he built an obstacle course. It was on a lake. His father pulled him with a snowmobile. He needed to go fast.

Ice cross downhill skaters train in different ways. But they all need great skating skills. They need good balance.

Ice cross downhill is an extreme winter sport.

Ice cross downhill is like ski cross. Ski cross is a timed racing event. Four skiers start at the same time. They compete. Their track is 3,280 feet (1,000 m) long. It has jumps, waves, and steep turns.

"Ice cross downhill skaters train in different ways. But they all need great skating skills."

The ice cross downhill track is shorter and smaller than a ski-cross track.

3 Creating Champions

How did ice cross downhill develop? Who is Jasper Felder? Who is Arttu Pihlainen?

Ice cross downhill was invented in 2000. Austrian ice hockey players invented it. They wore ice skates. They went down a **bobsled** course. A bobsled is a sled used for racing.

A year later, a course was built. It was the first ice cross downhill contest. The course went through a fish market. It was in Stockholm, Sweden. Jasper Felder was the first ice cross downhill winner.

Felder has won many medals. He has seven victories.

He was undefeated for five years. He coached the Swedish ice cross downhill team.

More contests were held. Each year, the tracks got harder. More people participated in the sport. More people came to see the sport. Ice cross downhill was featured on television. It became popular.

In 2010, the first ice cross downhill world championship was held. Arttu Pihlainen was the first world champion.

Downhill skating is based on downhill in-line skating.

Extreme Ice Cross Downhill: Know the Lingo

Berm: a raised piece of land

Big air: leaving the ground for a couple of seconds of hang time

Bonk: bouncing off an object

Bucket: helmet

Gorilla turn: using the whole body to force a turn around

Hinge: falling downhill with great force

Hit: a takeoff point, used to catch air

Mitts: hands

Mogul: a small hard mound or bump of ice

Pylon: a slow skater

Slam: crashing or falling hard

Stack: landing a jump on a flat area

Stroking: moving forward and backward from one blade to another

Ice cross downhill is a fast-growing sport. It's popular in northern Europe and Canada.

He won the first four-stop world championship. The event took place in four different cities.

People want ice cross downhill to become a sport in the Winter Olympics. In 2014, the International Ice Cross Sports Federation was founded. This helped make the sport more official.

4

Skaters Versus Skiers

How is ice cross downhill like downhill skiing? How is it like ice hockey?

Some ice cross downhill skaters are downhill skiers. Some are ice hockey players.

Ice cross downhill is similar to downhill skiing. Skiers go downhill. They ski quickly. They move around objects. They make big jumps. Skiers tend to have lean bodies. This makes them faster.

Marco Dallago said, "Speed is something that skiers are used to. … That basic feel for speed that I got from skiing has definitely helped me with ice cross downhill." Skiers are used to speed. They're used to going downhill. This means they can focus on other things.

But he also supports ice hockey. He said, "Hockey gives you two really important skills: skating and dealing with body contact."

Some people debate about which sport is better for downhill skating: skiing or ice hockey.

Ice cross downhill is similar to ice hockey. Skaters use ice hockey gear. They ice-skate. They're pushy. Ice hockey players tend to have big bodies. This makes them stronger.

NAILED IT!

That Happened?!?

Sweden gets a lot of snow. It has a long winter season. Many cities are covered in snow and thick ice. People start doing crazy things when trapped inside for too long. Erik Sunnerheim is from Sweden. His nickname is "The Demon." He's a professional skier. He ice-skated around a frozen lake. But he used a chainsaw to drag him. He went much faster than he would on his legs. He put the chainsaw's teeth into the ice on the lake. He let it pull him around. He didn't break the ice. A chainsaw is a power tool. It's used to cut down trees, cut through concrete, and cut ice. It's powerful and dangerous. One wrong move and people can die or injure themselves. If he broke the ice, he could have drowned. Sunnerheim's stunt is called "chainsaw ice skating."

Ice cross downhill skaters combine many skills.

Martin Niefnecker played ice hockey. Now, he does ice cross downhill. He said, "You've got a small advantage if you are more accustomed to the high-speed downhill racing from skiing. … But every race track is different. And there are some tracks where your skating style and skills are far more important."

Top downhill skaters need to ski and skate. They need to be fast, flexible, and tough.

5

No Pain, No Gain!

What are some risks of ice cross downhill? How do ice cross downhill skaters reduce risks?

Andrew Bergeson went through an obstacle course. He made a sharp turn. He saw others crash into walls. He jumped over two back-to-back humps. He landed on his second try. He said, "Bodies fly. Crashes happen. But there's no time to think."

Bergeson loves ice cross downhill. He said, "It incorporates all the things I like: hitting people, skating, and fast speeds." He played ice hockey and football.

He does a lot of downhill training. He goes down hills. He

hits every bump. He said, "We had some pretty **epic** wipeouts." Epic means big and awesome. Crashing is part of downhill skating.

Ice cross downhill skaters take a lot of risks. They make 33-foot (10 m) jumps. They skate at high speeds. They face three other skaters. They all want to finish first.

Ice cross downhill skaters practice going downhill. They practice crashing.

Ice cross downhill skaters need to be ready for anything.

The tracks are narrow and winding. There are many high-speed crashes. Bodies fly in the air. Limbs get tangled. Helmets bash against walls.

Christian Papillon was an ice cross downhill skater. He tore **ligaments** in his knee. Ligaments hold bones together. He stopped competing. He became the director of Crashed Ice. Crashed Ice is a downhill skating contest. He said,

"There is no place, no time, to be unfocused, not even for half a second."

Ice cross downhill skaters try to reduce risks. They practice. They prepare.

NAILED IT!

When Extreme Is Too Extreme!

Underwater ice hockey is also called sub-aqua ice hockey. It's played underneath the ice! It's played underneath frozen pools or ponds. It's played on a rink that's 20 feet (6 m) wide and 26 feet (8 m) long. It's played upside down. Players wear diving masks. They wear fins. They wear wetsuits. They do not have breathing gear. They come to the surface every 30 seconds to breathe. They cut out a square hole in the thick ice. They jump into the ice-cold water. They jump with their hockey sticks. They guide a floating puck into their opponents' goal. Four divers have oxygen tanks. They supervise every match. Underwater ice hockey periods last 10 minutes. Players are allowed 10-minute breaks to warm up. It started in Austria. It's more extreme than ice hockey and underwater hockey. Underwater hockey players use the floor of a swimming pool. They use a sinking puck.

Jordan Lalor builds his ice skating skills. He plays ice hockey. He Rollerblades. He snowboards.

Stephanie Fedoruk plays ice hockey. She runs. She studies the tracks. She watches how the track is built.

Matt Kawahara tried out for Crashed Ice three times. Once, he missed by less than a second. He trained more. He plays in three hockey leagues. He runs outdoors. He gets used to the cold air.

Ice cross downhill skaters are unstoppable.

"Matt Kawahara tried out for Crashed Ice three times."

Ice cross downhill skaters train for their racing events.

Did You Know?

- The world's first ice cross downhill training center is in Finland. It's at Serena Ski in Espoo.
- The oldest known ice skates were found at the bottom of a lake. The lake is in Switzerland. The ice skates were made in 3000 BCE. They were made from cattle bones.
- King James II of England and King Louis XIV of France loved ice skating. They built large ice skating rinks. The rinks were on their palace grounds.
- Ice blocking is another extreme ice sport. Many people ice block in the summer. But it can be done any time of the year. People go to the top of a hill. They sit or lie down on a large ice block. They slide down the hill. They keep sliding until the ice melts.
- Ice is the solid form of water. It covers 10 percent of Earth's land. It forms 7 percent of the oceans.
- Ice hockey fans in Detroit throw octopuses on the ice. They do this to celebrate winning a game. This tradition started in 1952.
- Women ice cross downhill skaters have their own contests in Crashed Ice. About 20 to 25 women compete in each race. The men's race portion includes a point system and final round. The women only have one chance to beat the fastest time.

Consider This!

TAKE A POSITION! Reread chapter four. Do you think ice cross downhill skaters benefit from being ice hockey players or downhill skiers? Which skill do you think is more important, skating or skiing? Argue your point with reasons and evidence.

SAY WHAT? Ice cross downhill has been compared to ice hockey, downhill skiing, ski cross, in-line skating, and NASCAR racing. Learn more about one of these sports. Explain how the two are similar and different.

THINK ABOUT IT! Most of the ice cross downhill tracks are built in cities. The track uses the city's features. It weaves through buildings and trees. What do you think are the pros and cons of this? How would you feel if you were a resident of the city? Would you like your city to host an event? Why or why not?

SEE A DIFFERENT SIDE! Some people think that women shouldn't do ice cross downhill. Explain their perspective.

Learn More: Resources

PRIMARY SOURCES

Ice Cross Downhill videos: http://www.redbull.com/us/en/snow/ice-cross-downhill/videos

SECONDARY SOURCES

Browning, Kurt, and Melanie Rose, illustrator. *A Is for Axel: An Ice Skating Alphabet*. Ann Arbor, MI: Sleeping Bear Press, 2006.

WEB SITES

International Ice Cross Sports Federation: http://worldicecrossleague.com/iicsf/

Red Bull Crashed Ice: www.redbullcrashedice.com

World Ice Cross Association: www.worldicecross.com

Glossary

bobsled (BAHB-sled) a sled used for racing

epic (EP-ik) big and crazy

exhausting (ig-ZAWST-eng) tiring

hairpin (HAIR-pin) sharp U-turn

ligaments (LIG-uh-mehntz) tissues in your body that hold bones together

Index